Incidence of Chytrid Fungus, *Batrachochytrium dendrobatidis*, in Southeast Coast Network Parks

Natural Resource Technical Report NPS/SECN/NRTR—2011/477

Michael W. Byrne and Marylou N. Moore

USDI National Park Service
Southeast Coast Inventory and Monitoring Network
Cumberland Island National Seashore
101 Wheeler Street
Saint Marys, Georgia 31558

August 2011

U.S. Department of the Interior
National Park Service
Natural Resource Stewardship and Science
Fort Collins, Colorado

The National Park Service, Natural Resource Stewardship and Science office in Fort Collins, Colorado publishes a range of reports that address natural resource topics of interest and applicability to a broad audience in the National Park Service and others in natural resource management, including scientists, conservation and environmental constituencies, and the public.

The Natural Resource Data Series is intended for the timely release of basic data sets and data summaries. Care has been taken to assure accuracy of raw data values, but a thorough analysis and interpretation of the data has not been completed. Consequently, the initial analyses of data in this report are provisional and subject to change.

All manuscripts in the series receive the appropriate level of peer review to ensure that the information is scientifically credible, technically accurate, appropriately written for the intended audience, and designed and published in a professional manner.

This report received formal peer review by subject-matter experts who were not directly involved in the collection, analysis, or reporting of the data. Data were collected and analyzed using established methods based on peer-reviewed protocols and were analyzed and interpreted within the guidelines of the protocols.

Views, statements, findings, conclusions, recommendations, and data in this report do not necessarily reflect views and policies of the National Park Service, U.S. Department of the Interior. Mention of trade names or commercial products does not constitute endorsement or recommendation for use by the U.S. Government.

This report is available from the Southeast Coast Network (http://science.nature.nps.gov/im/units/secn) and the Natural Resource Publications Management website (http://www.nature.nps.gov/publications/nrpm).

Please cite this publication as:

NPS 964/109152, August 2011

Contents

Contents (continued)

Figures

Tables

Abstract

A chytrid fungus, *Batrachochytrium dendrobatidis* (Bd), has been established as a causal factor in localized amphibian-population declines and extinctions around the world. The amphibian community in the Southeastern U.S. is widely considered to be one of the most diverse in the world, and is a valued resource in Southeast Coast Network (SECN) parks. In 2005, the SECN and the Savannah River Ecology Laboratory (SREL) began surveying for Bd occurrences in Chattahoochee National Recreation Area and Congaree National Park. Preliminary results indicated the fungus was present in these parks, which prompted further sampling efforts in other SECN parks. These efforts led to the identification of several new Bd occurrences, including the first record of Bd in Alabama and the first record in a species not known to host the fungus; results indicative of our current lack of knowledge of Bd distribution and species-specific susceptibility. The fungus was detected in four species: *Lithobates catesbeiana* (American bullfrog), *Lithobates sphenocephalus* (southern leopard frog), *Lithobates palustris* (pickerel frog), and *Eurycea cirrigera* (southern two-lined salamander). No evidence of the disease caused by Bd infection, chytridiomycosis, was observed. The objective of this initial survey was solely to document the occurrence of Bd within the SECN, therefore individual and population level effects remain unknown. Survey and monitoring efforts are ongoing to determine other species that are affected, and if Bd is having negative impacts on amphibian communities in the SECN.

Acknowledgements

The field component of this project was a joint endeavor by the SECN and the Savannah River Ecology Laboratory (SREL), under Cooperative Agreement #2114040022. Under this agreement, SREL collected samples at CAHA, CALO, CANA, and MOCR, overseen by W. Gibbons, J. Greene, and B. Rothermel. The SECN collected samples at CUIS, HOBE, KEMO, OCMU and TIMU/FOCA. The Bd findings at CHAT and CONG were opportunistically realized during the SECN-wide herpetofaunal inventories conducted by SREL under Cooperative Agreement #5028010262. The herpetofaunal inventory results were published in Tuberville et al. (2005) and the Bd findings at CHAT and CONG, among many other non NPS properties, were published in Rothermel et al. (2008). The authors wish to thank D. Calhoun, J. Barichivich, and C. Jones for their detailed review and excellent feedback, D. Lagana, E. Davie, B. Blankley, J. Maxfield, J. Mitchell, J. Hall, and S. Walls for assistance with fieldwork, and NPS Park staff, particularly J. Cahill, G. Lachine, W. Johnson, J. Fry, and R. Bryant, for their cooperation above and beyond the call of duty.

Introduction

The Southeastern U.S. is host to one of the most diverse amphibian communities in the world. With an estimated 140 amphibian species, more than half of which are salamanders, the Southeast accounts for about half of the total number of amphibians in the U.S. (Echternacht & Harris 1993, Petranka 1998). The Southeast Coast Network (SECN) consists of 20 National Parks that encompass more than 184,000 acres of federally-managed land throughout Florida, Georgia, Alabama, South Carolina, and North Carolina. Sixty-one amphibian species are confirmed to occur in SECN parks; 26 in Caudata, and 35 in Anura (NPSpecies 2011; Table 1).

A chytrid fungus, *Batrachochytrium dendrobatidis* (Bd), and the disease caused by this fungal pathogen, chytridiomycosis, has been linked to amphibian-population declines and extinctions around the world (Daszak et al. 2003, Muths et al. 2003, Briggs et al. 2005, Skerratt et al. 2007). Although variable, once infection progresses to chytridiomycosis, it generally kills 50–80% of infected individuals (Lips et al. 2003, Hossack et al. 2009), although it has been well documented to cause 100% mortality in several species (Lips et al. 2003, 2006). The extent of mortality is dependent upon local environmental conditions, stage of metamorphosis and mass (Tobler and Schmidt 2010), overall fitness, and, very likely, concomitant stressors. This pathogenic fungus was first identified in 1997 (Longcore et al. 1999), and in just over a decade, has been detected on every continent with the exception of Antarctica, which does not host amphibians (Fisher et al. 2009).

The fungus affects (i.e., feeds upon) keratinized portions of amphibian skin, such as ventral surfaces, feet, and mouthparts. Because amphibian skin is a vital organ that plays critical roles in respiration, osmoregulation, thermoregulation, and protection from pathogens such as viruses and bacteria (Duellman and Trueb 1986, Voyles et al. 2007), compromised skin can rapidly lead to death in an amphibian. The fungi become encysted in infected cells, causing lesions, discoloration, and hyperkeratosis (skin thickening; Berger et al. 1998). In addition to the aforementioned issues, infection also leads to electrolyte imbalance and significantly impaired cardiac function (Voyles et al. 2007).

Until relatively recently, it was widely believed that Bd was strictly an aquatic fungus with zoospores remaining viable in lake water for up to seven weeks (Johnson and Speare 2003); consequently, only amphibians with an aquatic stage were deemed to be at risk. DiRosa et al. (2007), however, identified an encysted form of Bd that is likely able to persist in the environment for much longer periods, although viability of this form was unknown. Further, Cummer et al. (2005) found Bd in a strictly terrestrial salamander, the Jemez Mountains salamander (*Plethodon neomexicanus*), in the southwestern U.S. While intraspecific contact with an infected individual was proposed as the likely cause of this incident, it appears obvious that Bd has many possible vectors for transmission across the landscape (e.g., water, animal migrations/movements, pet trade, reservoir species) and the fungus possesses one or more means for long-term persistence in the absence of a host (e.g., a resting stage, abiotic reservoir; Di Rosa et al. 2007, Mitchell et al. 2008).

A variety of factors, including temperature and precipitation, influence the prevalence of Bd infection (Ron 2005). Cooler temperatures and moister conditions are correlated with an increase in prevalence (Retallick et al. 2004, Kriger and Hero 2006, 2007). In culture, Bd can grow in a wide range of temperatures, from 4–25°C (39–77°F; Piotrowski et al. 2004). The optimal temperature for maximum growth, however, is between 17°C (63°F) and 25°C, with 23°C (73°F) identified as the optimal temperature for growth (Piotrowski et al. 2004). The fungus grows very slowly or not at all below 10°C (50°F) or above 28°C (82°F; Piotrowski et al. 2004). Low temperatures can considerably reduce the production and activity levels of a variety of immune cells and proteins in amphibians (Rohr and Raffel 2010). Further, low temperatures also reduce the amount of antimicrobial skin peptides, which are known to be important for defending against Bd (Woodhams et al. 2007, Kilpatrick et al. 2010).

Given the general environmental conditions required of the fungus, our knowledge of the environmental conditions at SECN parks, our planned sampling effort, and the fundamental niche predictive model generated by Ron (2005), we initially did not expect Bd to occur at a high enough prevalence to be detected in the southern coastal SECN parks [i.e., Canaveral National Seashore (CANA), Castillo De San Marcos National Monument / Fort Matanzas National Monument (CASA/FOMA), Cumberland Island National Seashore (CUIS), Fort Frederica National Monument (FOFR), Fort Pulaski National Monument (FOPU), and Timucuan Ecological and Historic Preserve / Fort Caroline National Memorial (TIMU/FOCA)] (Figure 1). New Bd detections in Florida (Rizkalla 2009, 2010) since the time of this study, however, have caused us to reevaluate this hypothesis, although this is not the focus of this paper. We did, however, expect a higher likelihood of Bd detection in SECN's northern parks [i.e., Cape Hatteras National Seashore (CAHA), Cape Lookout National Seashore (CALO), Moores Creek National Battlefield (MOCR), Congaree National Park (CONG), Chattahoochee National recreation Area (CHAT), Kennesaw Mountain National Battlefield Park (KEMO), Ocmulgee National Monument (OCMU), and Horseshoe Bend National Military Park (HOBE)] (Figure 1), despite sample size limitations.

Although the fungus is considered to be highly contagious, has known adverse impacts on many species, and suspected low-host specificity, little was known at the outset of this work about occurrences of Bd in the southeastern U.S. During the herpetofaunal inventories of SECN parks conducted by Savannah River Ecology Laboratory (SREL; Tuberville et al. 2005), Bd samples were collected from several frogs at CONG and CHAT (Figure 1). The fungus was detected at both CONG and CHAT (Rothermel et al. 2008), thus prompting us, in 2005, to combine a Bd survey with other SECN monitoring work. Since that time, and the results of the project presented in this paper, a tremendous amount of work has occurred on Bd. The fungus has now been detected in several species in all states in the SECN (i.e., AL, FL, GA, NC, and SC) and adjacent states (i.e., AR, LA, TN, and VA; Table 2).

Objectives
The objectives of this project were:

1) Determine the host associations for *Batrachochytrium dendrobatidis* in SECN parks.

2) Determine prevalence of *Batrachochytrium dendrobatidis* infections in host species in SECN parks

Table 1. Amphibian species known to occur in SECN parks (NPSpecies 2011). Bd samples were collected from those species in bold.

Family	Scientific Name	Common Name	CAHA	CALO	CANA	CONG	CHAT	CUIS	HOBE	KEMO	MOCR	OCMU	TIMU/FOCA
Bufonidae	***Anaxyrus americanus***	**American toad**	X	X			X		X	X	X	X	
Bufonidae	***Anaxyrus fowleri***	**Fowler's toad**	X	X			X		X	X	X	X	
Bufonidae	*Anaxyrus quercicus*	Oak toad		X	X								
Bufonidae	***Anaxyrus terrestris***	**Southern toad**			X	X	X	X	X	X	X	X	X
Hylidae	***Acris crepitans***	**Northern cricket frog**				X	X		X	X		X	
Hylidae	***Acris gryllus***	**Southern cricket frog**		X	X	X		X	X		X	X	X
Hylidae	***Hyla avivoca***	**Bird-voiced treefrog**	X			X			X		X	X	
Hylidae	*Hyla chrysoscelis*	Cope's Gray treefrog	X	X	X	X	X	X	X	X	X	X	X
Hylidae	***Hyla cinerea***	**Green treefrog**	X	X	X	X	X	X	X	X	X	X	X
Hylidae	*Hyla femoralis*	Pine woods treefrog			X	X		X	X		X		X
Hylidae	*Hyla gratiosa*	Barking treefrog			X	X		X	X		X		X
Hylidae	***Hyla squirella***	**Squirrel treefrog**	X	X	X	X	X	X	X		X	X	X
Hylidae	*Hyla versicolor*	Gray treefrog	X			X			X	X			
Hylidae	*Pseudacris brachyphona*	Mountain chorus frog											
Hylidae	*Pseudacris brimleyi*	Brimley's chorus frog				X							
Hylidae	*Pseudacris crucifer*	Spring peeper			X	X	X	X	X	X	X	X	X
Hylidae	*Pseudacris crucifer crucifer*	Northern spring peeper					X		X	X	X		
Hylidae	*Pseudacris feriarum*	Southeastern chorus frog				X	X		X	X	X		
Hylidae	*Pseudacris nigrita*	Southern chorus frog			X	X						X	
Hylidae	*Pseudacris ocularis*	Little Grass frog	X	X	X			X			X	X	X
Hylidae	*Pseudacris ornata*	Ornate chorus frog				X					X	X	
Leptodactylidae	*Eleutherodactylus planirostris*	Greenhouse frog			X								X
Microhylidae	***Gastrophryne carolinensis***	**Eastern narrow-mouthed toad**	X	X	X	X	X	X	X		X	X	X
Ranidae	*Lithobates capito*	Gopher frog			X		X	X	X		X	X	X

3

Table 1. Continued.

Family	Scientific Name	Common Name	CAHA	CALO	CANA	CONG	CHAT	CUIS	HOBE	KEMO	MOCR	OCMU	TIMU/FOCA
Ranidae	*Lithobates catesbeianus*	Bullfrog	X			X	X		X	X	X	X	X
Ranidae	*Lithobates clamitans*	Green frog				X	X	X	X	X	X	X	X
Ranidae	*Lithobates clamitans clamitans*	Bronze frog				X						X	X
Ranidae	*Lithobates grylio*	Pig frog			X			X					X
Ranidae	*Lithobates heckscheri*	River frog				X							
Ranidae	*Lithobates palustris*	Pickerel frog				X	X		X	X	X	X	
Ranidae	*Lithobates sphenocephalus*	Southern leopard frog	X		X	X	X	X	X	X	X	X	X
Ranidae	*Lithobates sylvatica*	Wood frog							X				
Ranidae	*Lithobates virgatipes*	Carpenter frog				X							
Scaphiopodidae	*Scaphiopus holbrookii*	Eastern spadefoot		X	X	X	X	X	X		X		X
Ambystomatidae	*Ambystoma mabeei*	Mabee's salamander		X									
Ambystomatidae	*Ambystoma maculatum*	Spotted salamander				X	X	X	X	X			
Ambystomatidae	*Ambystoma opacum*	Marbled salamander				X	X	X	X	X	X	X	
Ambystomatidae	*Ambystoma talpoideum*	Mole salamander				X	X	X	X		X	X	X
Amphiumidae	*Amphiuma means*	Two-toed amphiuma	X					X		X		X	
Plethodontidae	*Desmognathus auriculatus*	Southern dusky salamander			X	X		X		X	X	X	
Plethodontidae	*Desmognathus fuscus*	Northern dusky salamander					X	X	X	X	X	X	
Plethodontidae	*Desmognathus monticola*	Seal salamander					X		X	X			
Plethodontidae	*Eurycea cirrigera*	Southern two-lined salamander				X	X		X	X	X	X	
Plethodontidae	*Eurycea guttolineata*	Three-lined salamander				X	X		X	X	X	X	
Plethodontidae	*Eurycea quadridigitata*	Dwarf salamander						X					
Plethodontidae	*Gyrinophilus porphyriticus*	Spring salamander					X		X	X			
Plethodontidae	*Plethodon chlorobryonis*	Atlantic coast slimy salamander	X			X							X

Table 1. Continued.

Family	Scientific Name	Common Name	CAHA	CALO	CANA	CONG	CHAT	CUIS	HOBE	KEMO	MOCR	OCMU	TIMU/FOCA
Plethodontidae	*Plethodon cinereus*	Eastern red-backed salamander	X										
Plethodontidae	***Plethodon glutinosus***	**Slimy salamander**					X		X		X		
Plethodontidae	*Plethodon grobmani*	Southeastern slimy salamander									X		X
Plethodontidae	***Plethodon ocmulgee***	**Ocmulgee slimy salamander**										X	
Plethodontidae	***Plethodon serratus***	**Southern red-backed salamander**					X			X			
Plethodontidae	*Plethodon websteri*	Southern zig-zag salamander								X			
Plethodontidae	*Pseudotriton montanus*	Mud salamander				X			X				
Plethodontidae	***Pseudotriton ruber***	**Red salamander**					X		X	X		X	
Proteidae	*Necturus punctatus*	Dwarf waterdog				X		X					
Salamandridae	*Notophthalmus perstriatus*	Striped newt			X			X					X
Salamandridae	*Notophthalmus viridescens*	Eastern newt		X	X		X		X				X
Sirenidae	*Siren intermedia*	Dwarf siren, lesser siren			X						X		
Sirenidae	*Siren lacertina*	Greater siren			X	X					X		

5

Table 2. Confirmed occurrences of *Batrachochytrium dendrobatidis* in wild-caught species in the Southeastern U.S (AL, AR, FL, GA, LA, MS, NC, SC, TN, VA).

Scientific Name	Common Name	Species Known to Occur in ≥ 1 SECN Park	Southeastern States with Confirmed Bd Occurrence
Anura			
Acris crepitans	Northern cricket frog	Y	AR[15], LA[15], VA[11]
Acris gryllus dorsalis	Florida cricket frog	N[A]	FL[13,14]
Anaxyrus americanus	American toad	Y	VA[11]
Anaxyrus fowleri	Fowler's toad	Y	VA[11]
Anaxyrus terrestris	Southern toad	Y	FL[14]
Anaxyrus sp.	Unknown *Anaxyrus* species	-	TN[4]
Eleutherodactylus planirostris	Greenhouse frog[B]	Y	FL[14]
Hyla chrysoscelis	Cope's gray treefrog	Y	VA[11]
Hyla versicolor/chrysoscelis	Gray treefrog/Cope's gray treefrog	Y	LA[15]
Lithobates catesbeianus	American bullfrog	Y	GA[7,15], SC[12], NC[15], VA[9,11,15]
Lithobates clamitans	Green frog	Y	GA[15,16], AL[3], LA[15], NC[5], VA[11]
Lithobates palustris	Pickerel frog	Y	GA[15,16], SC[15], TN[17]
Lithobates sp.	Unknown *Lithobates* species	-	GA[15]
Lithobates sphenocephalus	Southern leopard frog	Y	LA[15], GA[15,16], TN[18], NC[15], AR[15], VA[11]
Lithobates sylvaticus	Wood frog	Y	GA[15], TN[4]
Pseudacris crucifer	Spring peeper	Y	LA[15], VA[11]
Pseudacris fouquettei	Cajun chorus frog	N	LA[15]
Pseudacris ocularis	Little grass frog	Y	FL[14]
Pseudacris sp.	Unknown *Pseudacris* species	-	TN[4]
Caudata			
Cryptobranchus alleganiensis	Eastern hellbender	N	GA[6], AR[2]
Desmognathus conanti	Spotted dusky salamander	N	GA[16]

A. Species occurs but not this subspecies. B. Non-native. 1. Bakkegard & Pessier (2010). 2. Briggler et al. (2008). 3. Byrne et al. (2008). 4. Chatfield et al. (2009). 5. Chinnadurai et al. (2009). 6. Gonynor et al (2011). 7. Green & Dodd (2007). 8. Hossack et al. (2010). 9. Mitchell & Green (2002). 10. Montanucci (2009). 11. Petersen et al. (2011). 12. Peterson et al. (2007). 13. Rizkalla (2009). 14. Rizkalla (2010). 15. Rothermel et al. (2008). 16. Timpe et al. (2008). 17. Todd-Thompson et al. (2009). 18. Venesky & Brem (2008)

Table 2. Continued.

Scientific Name	Common Name	Species Known to Occur in ≥1 SECN Park	Southeastern States with Confirmed Bd Occurrence
Desmognathus fuscus	Northern dusky salamander	Y	VA[11]
Desmognathus monticola	Seal salamander	Y	VA[8]
Eurycea cirrigera	Southern two-lined salamander	Y	AL[3], GA[16]
Eurycea longicauda	Long-tailed salamander	N	VA[11]
Notophthalmus viridescens dorsalis	Broken-striped newt	N[A]	NC[15]
Notophthalmus viridescens viridescens	Eastern newt	Y	AL[1], GA[15], VA[15], TN[4]
Plethodon glutinosus	Northern slimy salamander	Y	NC[5]
Plethodon yonahlossee	Yonahlossee salamander	N	NC[5]
Pseudotriton ruber	Northern red salamander	Y	SC[10], VA[11]

A. Species occurs but not this subspecies. B. Non-native. 1. Bakkegard & Pessier (2010). 2. Briggler et al. (2008). 3. Byrne et al. (2008). 4. Chatfield et al. (2009). 5. Chinnadurai et al. (2009). 6. Gonynor et al. (2011). 7. Green & Dodd (2007). 8. Hossack et al. (2010). 9. Mitchell & Green (2002). 10. Montanucci (2009). 11. Petersen et al. (2011). 12. Peterson et al. (2007). 13. Rizkalla (2009). 14. Rizkalla (2010). 15. Rothermel et al. (2008). 16. Timpe et al. (2008). 17. Todd-Thompson et al. (2009). 18. Venesky & Brem (2008)

Methods

Study Area

As previously mentioned, an opportunistic survey conducted during the herpetofaunal inventories by the SREL occurred at CHAT and CONG. Subsequent to this initial effort, the Southeast Coast Network parks in the broader survey summarized herein are CAHA, CALO, CANA, CUIS, MOCR, HOBE, KEMO, OCMU, and the jointly-managed TIMU/FOCA (Figure 1). The Bd survey location, data collector, collection season, target taxa, and sample type collected are summarized in Table 3.

Parks were selected based upon a) estimated high amphibian diversity, b) estimated high relative abundance, c) efficient access across the park, and d) variability in amphibian habitat types. Randomization, and subsequent park-wide levels of inference, was not incorporated into this survey as a means to most effectively address the objectives and aforementioned criteria. Sampling effort was approximately equally distributed across each park in an attempt to adequately characterize all park lands, including within and across habitat types considered suitable amphibian habitat (i.e., not salt marshes).

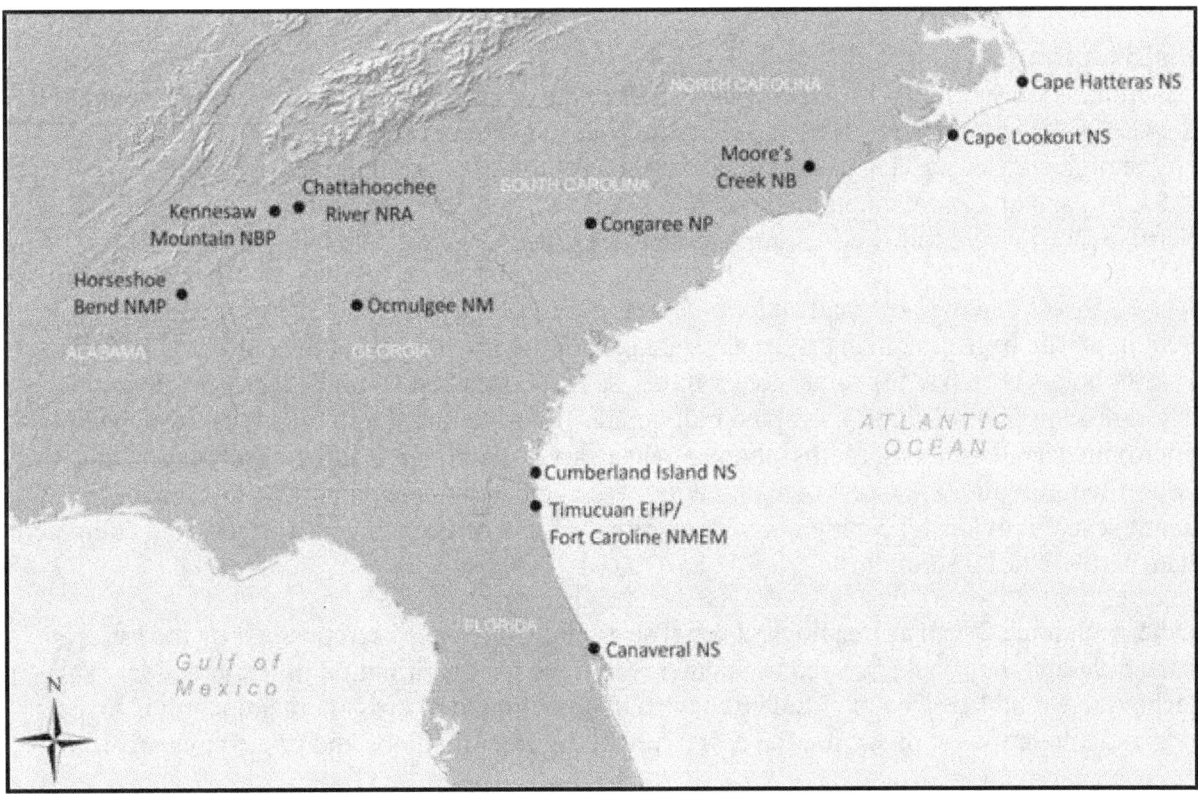

Figure 1. SECN parks preliminarily surveyed for presence of the chytrid fungus *Batrachochytrium dendrobatidis*, 2005–2008.

Table 3. Bd survey location, data collector, collection season, target taxa, and sample type.

Location	Collector	Season & Year	Target	Sample Type
CAHA	SREL	Fall 2007	Anura	Pooled, Individual
CALO	SREL	Summer 2008	Anura	Individual
CANA	SREL	Summer 2008	Anura	Individual
CHAT	SREL	Spring 2005	Anura	Individual
CONG	SREL	Spring 2005	Anura	Individual
CUIS	SECN	Spring 2006	Anura	Pooled
HOBE	SECN	Spring 2006, Fall 2006	Anura, Caudata	Pooled, Individual
KEMO	SECN	Spring 2006, Fall 2006	Anura, Caudata	Pooled, Individual
MOCR	SREL	Fall 2007	Anura, Caudata	Pooled, Individual
OCMU	SECN	Spring 2006, Fall 2006	Anura, Caudata	Pooled, Individual
TIMU/FOCA	SECN	Spring 2006	Anura, Caudata	Pooled

Targeted Species

All species that were encountered were sampled for Bd. The SREL team focused on members of the Family Ranidae, but a few samples in other Anuran families were also collected. The SECN team collected samples across the orders Anura and Caudata.

Field Methods

All animals were handled in accordance with the care and use guidelines set forth in ASIH / HL / SSAR (2004) [American Society of Ichthyologists and Herpetologists (ASIH), The Herpetologists' League (HL). and the Society for the Study of Amphibians and Reptiles (SSAR)], and all decontamination procedures outlined in NSW National Parks and Wildlife Service (2001) were followed. Sample-collection procedures are detailed in Byrne (2007).

Animals were captured by hand and dip-nets (Figure 2). Captured animals were individually held in plastic bags or containers, processed, and released at the point of capture within 36 hours. If sampling occurred at the same site on more than one occasion, animals were toe-clipped to avoid re-sampling previously sampled individuals. Each captured individual was swabbed approximately 15–20 times across the ventral surfaces, mouthparts, and toe webbing with a cotton swab (Figure 2). Cross contamination was avoided by using a new pair of gloves to handle each individual, keeping individuals separate, and disinfecting all surfaces and equipment with a 10% NaClO solution.

Other techniques, such as histological serial sectioning, have not been pursued by the SECN to date, although they could be used as another technique for confirmation of Bd infection. This technique would likely be most suited to when the likelihood of cross-contamination is high or unavoidable; however this is not the case given our current methods and procedures regarding cross-contamination avoidance.

All sampled individuals were examined in the field superficially for any atypical or abnormal (potentially obvious) characteristics that could be suggestive of Bd infection. For example, lesions, skin discoloration, abnormal ecdysis, exudates, or general lethargy suggested through observation prior to capture or capture avoidance.

The SREL collected samples at CHAT and CONG in spring 2005 (Rothermel et al. 2008). Subsequent sample-collection by SREL occurred at MOCR and CAHA in fall 2007, and at CALO and CANA in summer 2008 (Table 3). The SECN collected samples at CUIS, HOBE, KEMO, OCMU, and TIMU/FOCA in early spring 2006, and at HOBE, KEMO, and OCMU in fall 2006 (Table 3).

Two stages of sample collection occurred at parks sampled by the SECN (i.e., CUIS, HOBE, KEMO, OCMU, TIMU/FOCA). An initial cursory collection event occurred in the spring of 2006 at CUIS, HOBE, KEMO, OCMU, and TIMU/FOCA. Samples pooled when possible to minimize travel and analysis costs. Follow-up and more intensive sampling efforts occurred in the fall of 2006 at HOBE, KEMO, and OCMU where individual samples were collected where either the previously pooled samples were positive or the results of the pooled samples were inconclusive. Follow-up sampling was conducted at HOBE, KEMO, and OCMU due to the inclusion of species in the previous pooled sample(s) that were not previously known hosts to Bd. Additionally, some sampling location(s) where previous collections occurred within the park were too close to one another or were of similar habitat types of similar ecological condition.

Both individual and pooled swab samples were stored in a 70% EtOH solution, with individual samples held in 2-mL vials, and pooled samples held in 50-mL vials. All pooled samples consisted of swab samples from ≤ 10 individuals of more than one species, aggregated into one sample vial. Only post-metamorphic amphibians were sampled at CUIS, OCMU, and TIMU/FOCA; however, samples were collected across metamorphic stages at CAHA, CALO, CANA, CHAT, CONG, HOBE, KEMO, and MOCR.

Figure 2. Sample collection: on the left is an example capture technique (dip-netting), and on the right is an example of the amphibian swabbing technique.

Laboratory Analysis

All samples were analyzed by Pisces Molecular, Boulder, Colorado. Liquid in each of the skin swab samples was mixed by pipetting the liquid up and down repeatedly. The entire volume of each sample was then transferred into individual microfuge tubes. The tubes were spun in a microcentrifuge at ~16,000 x G for 3 minutes. The supernatant was then drawn off and discarded, a lysis buffer was added to the tubes and any pellet present was re-suspended by vortexing, and 10 µg of carrier DNA was added to the lysis buffer. DNA was extracted from all samples using a spin-column DNA purification procedure. DNA extracted from swabs and alcohol were assayed for the presence of a 296 base pair fragment of the Bd ribosomal ribonucleic acid (RNA) Intervening Transcribed Sequence region by 45-cycle single-round polymerase chain reaction (PCR) amplification with an established assay developed by Seanna Annis and modified for greater specificity and sensitivity by Pisces Molecular (J. Wood, Pisces Molecular, pers. comm.). Each group of sample PCR reactions included the following control reactions: a) positive DNA (i.e., DNA prepared from a positively identified laboratory culture of Bd strain JEL 270 donated by Joyce Longcore previously demonstrated to be positive by PCR for the Bd target fragment); b) negative DNA (i.e., DNA prepared from a laboratory culture of a non-*Batrachochytrium*, chytrid fungus, previously demonstrated to be negative by PCR for Bd.); and c) no DNA (i.e., H_2O in place of template DNA, this reaction remains uncapped during addition of sample DNA to the test reactions and served as a control to detect contaminating DNA in the PCR reagents or carryover of positive DNA during reaction set-up). Although Pisces Molecular has an effective quantitative detection sensitivity (e.g., <0.1 zoospore/mL, J. Wood, pers. comm.; <0.23 zoospore/mL; Rothermel et al. 2008), results in this paper are presented qualitatively as "detected" and "not-detected". Given Pisces Molecular's detection sensitivity, we have strong confidence in the test results. Further, a quantitative summary (i.e., zoospore equivalents / count estimates) is not necessary to meet the objectives of this project.

Results

Batrachochytrium dendrobatidis Detection

Species sampled (Table 1), species compositions of pooled samples including positive and negative test results for Bd (Table 4), and summaries of individual samples (including pooled samples when pooled samples were monospecific: Table 5) indicate that, given the sample size, the pathogen was detected at four SECN parks (Figure 3).

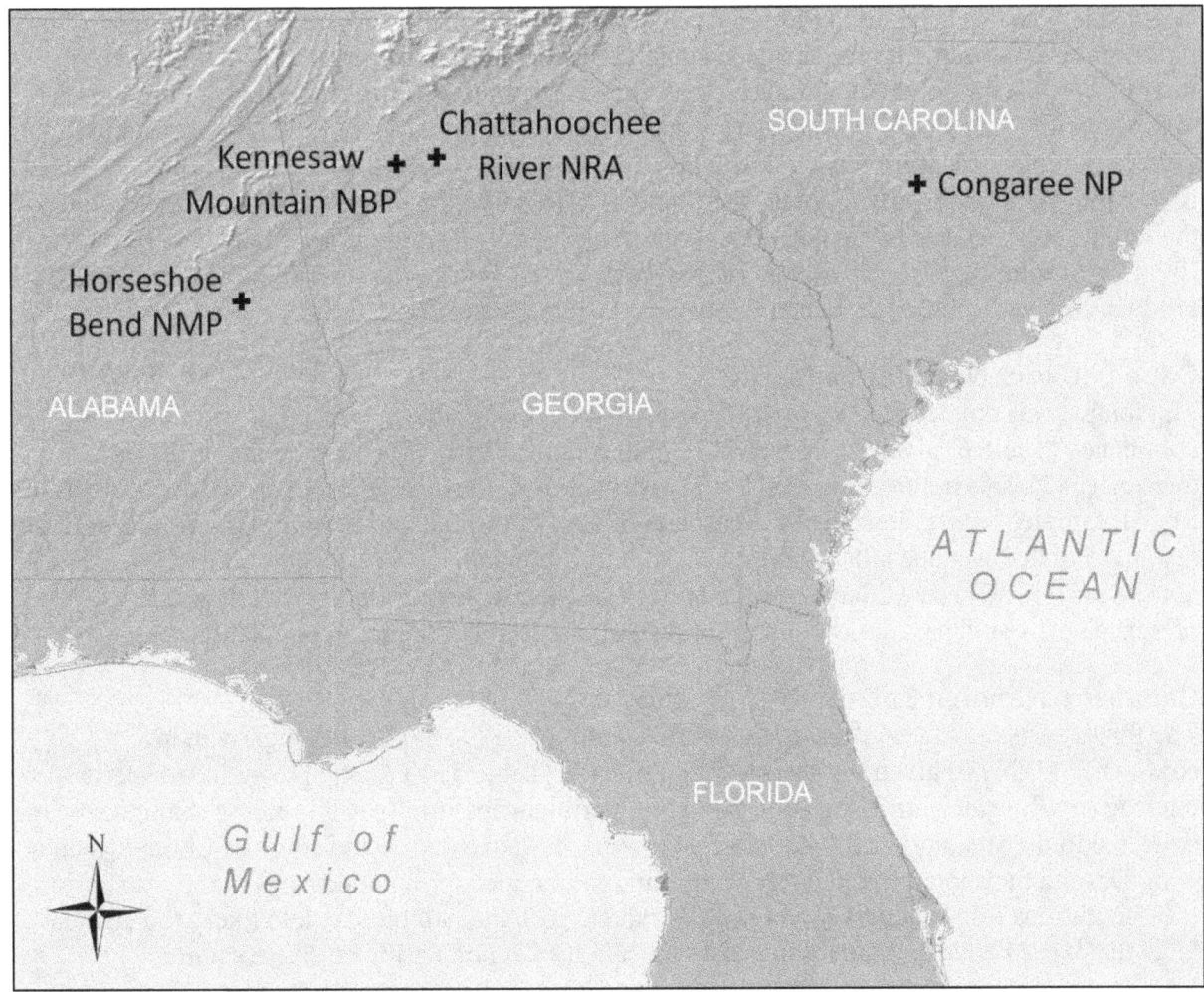

Figure 3. SECN parks with at least one individual testing positive for Bd during 2005-2008 sampling efforts.

The detection of any disease is a function of sample size, the accuracy of the test, and the prevalence of the disease in the population of interest. Methods developed by DiGiacomo and Koepsell (1986) were used to determine the confidence level of Bd detection, given the a) sample size (Table 5), b) an estimated conservative value for prevalence of Bd infection of 1%, and c) a test accuracy of 100%, that at least one infected individual is detected (Table 6). This was calculated for species and parks where a positive specimen was not collected. Although this method assumes a diagnostic accuracy of 100%, the sensitivity of the PCR analysis was <0.1 zoospore/mL (J. Wood, pers. comm.). The calculation of confidence levels followed: $C = 1 - (1$

$- p)^n$; where C = confidence level, p = estimated infection prevalence, n = sample size (DiGiacomo and Koepsell 1986). The sample sizes for each species were not pooled across parks as prevalence of the disease at any given location is specific to the sampling period, and likely varies depending on environmental conditions, and anthropogenic or other stressors. Sample sizes were inadequate to detect Bd for species where the fungus was not detected if the true prevalence of the pathogen in the population is estimated to be 1% (Table 5, Table 6). Confidence levels for Bd detection for most species were very low (i.e., less than 10%), with only a few species with confidence levels of approximately 25% [i.e., Northern dusky salamander / seal salamander (*Desmognathus fuscus/monticola*), slimy salamander (*Plethodon glutinosus*), and Southern red-backed salamander (*Plethodon serratus*) at KEMO, and green treefrog (*Hyla cinerea*) and Ocmulgee slimy salamander (*Plethodon ocmulgee*) at OCMU], yet still below 40% (Table 6). In summary, despite the seemingly large sample sizes for some species, sample sizes were inadequate at all parks sampled to detect Bd if the pathogen occurred in low prevalence (i.e., low frequency) or, although less likely given the biology of the fungus, if the fungus only occurred in isolated locations at each park. Sampling error may also be a factor if timing of sampling (i.e., season or year and associated environmental conditions) affects Bd productivity, and subsequent detection by surveys, at parks differentially.

Cape Lookout National Seashore
The fungus was not detected in species sampled at CALO (Table 1), although with low confidence (Table 6) given the sample size collected (Table 5). The sample included green treefrog (n=2), squirrel treefrog (n=7), and *Scaphiopus holbrookii* (Eastern spadefoot; n=8; Table 5). All samples were collected at the east end of Harkers Island and no sampling occurred in the few and isolated wetlands that occur on Shackleford Banks, North Core, and South Core islands at the Seashore. These wetlands are the only freshwater resources on the islands and Bd presence here could have a pronounced impact on the island amphibian population.

Canaveral National Seashore
The fungus was not detected in species sampled at CANA (Table 2), although with low confidence (Table 6) given the sample size collected (Table 5). The sample included green treefrog (n=9), squirrel treefrog (n=2), and Southern leopard frog (n=2; Table 5). Samples were collected in the area north of State Road 402, west of State Road 3, and south of County Road 406. Despite the short and relatively warm fall, winter, and spring conditions at the Seashore (i.e., conditions less conducive to high Bd productivity), the pathogen is less likely to persist at a level that would have dramatic impacts on the amphibian population at the Seashore.

Chattahoochee National Recreation Area (From Rothermel et al. 2008)
The fungus was detected in species sampled at CHAT (Table 1), although with low confidence (Table 6) given the sample size collected (Table 5). The sample included *Anaxyrus americanus* (American toad; n=1), postmetamorphic *Lithobates* spp. (n=18), and larval *Lithobates* spp. (n=39; Table 5). Two larvae and five postmetamorphic *Lithobates* spp. tested positive for Bd for an estimated prevalence of 12% (7/57, 95% CI: 3.8-20.8%; Table 5). Given the sample size, confidence level to detect Bd in species other than *Lithobates* spp. is low (Table 6). Rothermel et al. (2008) indicated that no obvious signs of the disease were observed. The majority of samples were collected in the Johnson Ferry Unit, which consists of vegetation / wetland communities and physical characteristics not typical of the Recreation Area as a whole.

Congaree National Park (from Rothermel et al. 2008)

The fungus was detected in species sampled at CONG (Table 1), although with low confidence (Table 6) given the sample size collected (Table 5). The sample included *Anaxyrus terrestris* (southern toad; n=1), postmetamorphic *Lithobates palustris* (pickerel frog; n=29), and unidentified *Lithobates* spp. (n=7; Table 5). Twenty-two of 29 post-metamorphic pickerel frog samples tested positive for Bd for an estimated prevalence of 76% (95% CI: 60.3-91.4%; Table 5). Given the sample size, confidence level to detect Bd for species other than pickerel frog is low (Table 6). Rothermel et al. (2008) indicated that no obvious signs of the disease were observed in the individuals sampled. Samples were collected at Weston Lake and along Sims Trail.

Cumberland Island National Seashore

The fungus was not detected in species sampled at CUIS (Table 1), although with low confidence (Table 6) given the sample size collected (Table 5). A pooled sample was collected at CUIS in spring 2006 (Table 4), and contained swab samples from 10 individual Southern leopard frogs (Table 5). Further, given the monospecific sample, it is unknown if Bd occurs in other species at CUIS. Samples were collected throughout the Seashore; specifically, White Cottage well, along the entirety of Willow Pond Trail, and along the entirety of North Cut Road.

Horseshoe Bend National Military Park

The fungus was detected in two species sampled (Table 1) during both sampling events that occurred at HOBE (spring and fall 2006; Table 4, Table 5).

Two pooled samples were collected at HOBE in spring 2006 (Table 4). One sample contained pooled swabs from *Eurycea cirrigera* (Southern two-lined salamander; n=9), *Eurycea guttolineata* (three-lined salamander; n=1), and the other pooled sample consisted of swabs from *Acris gryllus* (Southern cricket frog; n=2), *Lithobates clamitans* (green frog; n=3), and Southern leopard frog (n=3). Both pooled samples tested positive for Bd, but because the samples consisted of more than one species, the actual species(s) infected was undeterminable.

The fall 2006 sampling event consisted of collecting solely individual samples. The sample included Southern cricket frog (n=3), green frog (n=27), Northern dusky salamander (n=12), Southern two-lined salamander (n=50), three-lined salamander (n=7), larval *Gyrinophilus porphyriticus* (spring salamander; n=1), *Plethodon glutinosus* (slimy salamander; n=5), and *Pseudotriton ruber* (red salamander; n=1; Table 5). Although the fungus was detected in the individuals evaluated at HOBE, given the sample size (Table 5) low confidence was calculated (Table 6) to detect Bd in other amphibians other than Southern two-lined salamander and green frog. Samples were collected throughout the Park; specifically, in the beaver pond, all insular streams, and at least two locations along each stream that originated outside the park. All of the streambeds were predominantly sand and gravel.

The fungus was detected in 15% (4/27, 95% CI: 1.4-28.2) of the green frog samples, and 42% (21/50, 95% CI: 28.3-55.7) of the Southern two-lined salamander samples (Table 5). Although no obvious signs of the disease were observed in animals that tested positive for Bd, several infected Southern two-lined salamander were lethargic and their tails detached or were crushed during very light handling. In streams where these two species occurred together, some samples of each tested positive; however, positive samples for each species were also collected at locations where both species did not occur. Given the size of the park (approximately 825 ha), point-pattern analysis was unnecessary at this scale as it is assumed the fungus is evenly distributed across the park. The distribution of animals that tested positive for Bd supports this assumption.

Kennesaw Mountain National Battlefield Park

Several species were tested for Bd during both a spring and fall 2006 sampling event at KEMO (Table 1); however, the fungus was only detected in one individual of one species during the fall sampling event (Table 5). Although the fungus was detected (Table 5), it is with low confidence (Table 6) that an adequate representation of Bd occurrences at KEMO was identified given the sample size collected (Table 5). Individual samples were collected during both the spring and fall 2006 sampling events and are included in Table 5 and the calculations of Table 6.

The sample included Fowlers toad (n=1), bullfrog (n=1), Southern leopard frog (n=2), *Ambystoma maculatum* (spotted salamander; n=1), Northern dusky salamander or seal salamander, uncertain identification (n=48), Southern two-lined salamander (n=10), three-lined salamander (n=1), larval spring salamander (n=3), adult spring salamander (n=2), slimy salamander (n=30), Southern red-backed salamander (n=31), and red salamander (n=3; Table 5). Samples were collected throughout the Park; specifically, John Ward Creek and its tributaries, the east faces of Kennesaw Mountain and Little Kennesaw Mountain, Cheatham Hill, and Pigeon Hill (with some samples collected adjacent to seeps in these areas), and two small insular streams.

The one bullfrog sample, and the only sample testing positive for Bd collected at the Park, was collected from a dead specimen (Table 5). The bullfrog individual was found in a small 20-cm deep non-flowing pool (2m-x-4m) in an ephemeral stream where several other amphibians were sampled (e.g., Northern dusky salamander / seal salamander, Southern two-lined salamander, red salamander), none of which tested positive for the fungus. The dead individual was collected for later analysis to determine if death was attributable to chytridiomycosis; however no obvious signs of the disease were observed upon a cursory physical examination (i.e., lesions, skin discoloration, abnormal ecdysis, or any possible post-mortem exudates).

Moores Creek National Battlefield

The fungus was not detected in species sampled at MOCR (Table 1), although with low confidence (Table 6) given the sample size collected (Table 5). The sample was composed of both pooled (Table 4) and individual samples (Table 5). One pooled sample contained swab samples from three individual squirrel treefrogs, another pooled sample contained swab samples from four green treefrogs. The individual samples consisted of Southern leopard frog (n=2), green frog (n=1), Southern cricket frog (n=8), green treefrog (n=1), and southern toad (n=3; Table 5). Because the pooled samples were monospecific, the counts were combined and reported in Table 5 and the calculations in Table 6 were based upon the aggregated counts of pooled and individual samples. Samples were collected along the History Trail and Moores Creek.

Ocmulgee National Monument

Several species were tested for Bd during both a spring and fall 2006 sampling event at OCMU (Table 1); and the fungus was not detected at the Monument during either sampling event (Table 4, Table 5), although with low confidence (Table 6) given the sample size collected (Table 5).

One pooled sample was collected at OCMU in spring 2006 (Table 4). The sample contained pooled swabs from one Southern cricket frog and three green treefrogs (Table 4).

The fall 2006 sampling event consisted of collecting solely individual samples. The sample included *Acris crepitans* (Northern cricket frog; n=12), *Acris crepitans/gryllus* (Northern cricket frog or Southern cricket frog, uncertain identification; n=12), Southern cricket frog (n=5), Fowlers toad (n=1), Southern toad (n=1), *Gastrophryne carolinensis* (Eastern narrow-mouthed toad; n=2), *Hyla avivoca* (bird-voiced treefrog; n=1), green treefrog (n=44), green frog (n=5), *Ambystoma opacum* (marbled salamander; n=3), and Ocmulgee slimy salamander (n=28) (Table 5). Samples were collected throughout the Monument, including along the Ocmulgee River, adjacent wetlands, and tributaries, Walnut Creek, and the Opelofa, Heritage, and Loop Trails.

Timucuan Ecological and Historic Preserve / Fort Caroline National Memorial

Several species were tested for Bd in spring 2006 sampling event at TIMU/FOCA (Table 1); and the fungus was not detected at the Preserve/Memorial during either sampling event (Table 4, Table 5), although with low confidence (Table 6) given the sample size collected (Table 5).

Two pooled samples were collected at TIMU/FOCA in spring 2006 (Table 4). One sample contained pooled swabs from Eastern narrow-mouthed toad (n=1), green frog (n=2), and Southern leopard frog (n=3; Table 4), and the other pooled sample consisted of green frog (n=2), *Lithobates clamitans clamitans* (bronze frog; n=3), and Southern leopard frog (n=1; Table 4). Samples were collected in the southern part of the park, specifically the Theodore Roosevelt Area and Fort Caroline National Memorial.

Table 4. Pooled samples collected as part of this survey effort and species included in each pooled sample. Monospecific pooled samples are included in Tables 4 and 5. " – " = negative test result for Bd, " + " = positive test result for Bd.

Scientific Name	Common Name	Sample ID	Sample n	Park	Test Result
Lithobates sphenocephalus	Southern leopard frog	CH-1	10	CAHA	–
Lithobates catesbeianus	Bullfrog	CH-2	5	CAHA	–
Lithobates sphenocephalus	Southern leopard frog	CU-1	10	CUIS	–
[1]*Eurycea cirrigera*	Southern two-lined salamander	HO-1	9	HOBE	+
[1]*Eurycea guttolineata*	Three-lined salamander	HO-1	1	HOBE	+
[1]*Acris gryllus*	Southern cricket frog	HO-2	2	HOBE	+
[1]*Lithobates clamitans*	Green frog	HO-2	3	HOBE	+
[1]*Lithobates sphenocephalus*	Southern leopard frog	HO-2	3	HOBE	+
Hyla squirella	Squirrel treefrog	MO-1	3	MOCR	–
Hyla cinerea	Green treefrog	MO-2	4	MOCR	–
Acris gryllus	Southern cricket frog	OC-1	1	OCMU	–
Hyla cinerea	Green treefrog	OC-1	3	OCMU	–
Gastrophyne carolinensis	Eastern narrow-mouthed toad	TF-1	1	TIMU/FOCA	–
Lithobates clamitans	Green frog	TF-1	2	TIMU/FOCA	–
Lithobates sphenocephalus	Southern leopard frog	TF-1	3	TIMU/FOCA	–
Lithobates clamitans	Green frog	TF-2	2	TIMU/FOCA	–
Lithobates clamitans clamitans	Bronze frog	TF-2	3	TIMU/FOCA	–
Lithobates sphenocephalus	Southern leopard frog	TF-2	1	TIMU/FOCA	–

[1] Specific host species in sample testing positive for Bd indeterminate because pooled sample was composed of >1 species. See Sample ID.

Table 5. Amphibian species sampled for presence of *Batrachochytrium dendrobatidis*, sample size (includes monospecific pooled samples, see Table 2), percentage testing positive, and sample-collection site, 2005–2008.

Scientific Name	Number Testing Positive for *Batrachochytrium dendrobatidis* / Number Sampled (% Testing Positive)										
	CAHA	CALO	CANA	CONG	CHAT	CUIS	HOBE	KEMO	MOCR	OCMU	TIMU/FOCA
Anura											
Acris crepitans										0/12	
Acris crepitans/gryllus										0/12	
Acris gryllus							0/3		0/8	0/5	
Anaxyrus americanus					0/1						
Anaxyrus fowleri	0/3							0/1		0/1	
Anaxyrus terrestris				0/1					0/3	0/1	
Gastrophryne carolinensis										0/2	0/1
Hyla avivoca										0/1	
Hyla cinerea	0/3	0/2	0/9						0/5	0/44	
Hyla squirrella	0/2	0/7	0/2						0/3		

Table 5. Continued.

Scientific Name	Number Testing Positive for *Batrachochytrium dendrobatidis* / Number Sampled (% Testing Positive)										
	CAHA	CALO	CANA	CONG	CHAT	CUIS	HOBE	KEMO	MOCR	OCMU	TIMU/FOCA
Lithobates spp.					7/57[1] (12%)						
Lithobates catesbeianus	0/5			0/<7[2]				1/1 (100%)			
Lithobates clamitans				0/<7[2]			4/27 (15%)	0/1	0/1	0/5	0/4
Lithobates clamitans clamitans											0/1
Lithobates palustris				22/29 (76%)							
Lithobates sphenocephalus	0/15		0/2	0/<7		0/10	0/1	0/2	0/2		0/2
Scaphiopus holbrookii		0/8									
Caudata											
Ambystoma maculatum								0/1			
Ambystoma opacum										0/3	
Ambystoma talpoideum											0/1

[1] Sample composed of 18 postmetamorphic and 39 larval Ranids (Rothermel et al. 2008).
[2] Relative counts of *Lithobates catesbeianus, Lithobates clamitans, and Lithobates sphenocephalus* in the sample were not recorded by Rothermel et al. (2008) at CONG.

Table 5. Continued.

Scientific Name	CAHA	CALO	CANA	CONG	CHAT	CUIS	HOBE	KEMO	MOCR	OCMU	TIMU/FOCA
Desmognathus fuscus							0/12				
Desmognathus fuscus/monticola.								0/48			
Eurycea cirrigera							21/50 (42%)	0/10			
Eurycea guttolineata							0/7	0/1			
Gyrinophilus porphyriticus							0/1	0/5			
Plethodon glutinosus							0/5	0/30			
Plethodon ocmulgee										0/28	
Plethodon serratus								0/31			
Pseudotriton ruber							0/1	0/3			

Number Testing Positive for *Batrachochytrium dendrobatidis* / Number Sampled (% Testing Positive)

21

Table 6. Estimated confidence level that at least one infected individual would be detected (DiGiacoma and Koepsell 1986) given a) the sample sizes (Table 3), b) an estimated prevalence of *Batrachochytrium dendrobatidis* infection of 1%, and c) a test accuracy of 100% (although not attained). Calculated for species and locations where a positive specimen was not detected.

Scientific Name	Estimated Confidence Level of Detection if True Bd Prevalence is 1% (%)										
	CAHA	CALO	CANA	CONG	CHAT	CUIS	HOBE	KEMO	MOCR	OCMU	TIMU/FOCA
Anura											
Acris crepitans										11.4	
Acris crepitans/gryllus										11.4	
Acris gryllus							3.0		7.7	4.9	
Anaxyrus americanus					1.0						
Anaxyrus fowleri	3.0							1.0		1.0	
Anaxyrus terrestris				1.0					3.0	1.0	
Gastrophryne carolinensis										2.0	1.0
Hyla avivoca										1.0	
Hyla cinerea	3.0	2.0	8.6						4.9	35.7	
Hyla squirrella	2.0	6.8	2.0						3.0		

Table 6. Continued.

Scientific Name	Estimated Confidence Level of Detection if True Bd Prevalence is 1% (%)										
	CAHA	CALO	CANA	CONG	CHAT	CUIS	HOBE	KEMO	MOCR	OCMU	TIMU/FOCA
Lithobates spp.					NA						
Lithobates catesbeianus	4.9			6.8				NA			
Lithobates clamitans				6.8			NA	1.0	1.0	4.9	3.9
Lithobates clamitans clamitans											1.0
Lithobates palustris				NA							
Lithobates sphenocephalus	14.0		2.0	6.8		9.6	1.0	2.0	2.0		2.0
Scaphiopus holbrookii		7.7									
Caudata											
Ambystoma maculatum								1.0			
Ambystoma opacum										3.0	
Ambystoma talpoideum											1.0

Table 6. Continued.

Estimated Confidence Level of Detection if True Bd Prevalence is 1% (%)

Scientific Name	CAHA	CALO	CANA	CONG	CHAT	CUIS	HOBE	KEMO	MOCR	OCMU	TIMU/FOCA
Desmognathus fuscus							11.4				
Desmognathus fuscus/monticola								38.3			
Eurycea cirrigera							NA	9.6			
Eurycea guttolineata							6.8	1.0			
Gyrinophilus porphyriticus							1.0	4.9			
Plethodon glutinosus							4.9	26.0			
Plethodon ocmulgee										24.5	
Plethodon serratus								26.8			
Pseudotriton ruber							1.0	3.0			

24

Discussion

The SECN began surveying for Bd as part of our herpetological inventories in 2005. During the inventory, Bd was detected in two parks, and efforts were expanded to other SECN parks the following year. As part of the current survey, and the additional samples collected during the herpetofaunal inventories (Tuberville et al. 2005), four species have been identified as hosts to the fungal pathogen Bd in SECN parks. These species are: bullfrog, Southern leopard frog, pickerel frog, and Southern two-lined salamander (Figure 4). The presence of Bd in *Lithobates* pickerel frog at CONG is a notable finding, as this species is considered a Species of Special Concern by the state of South Carolina. The Bd finding in Southern two-lined salamander is also significant in that it is the first recorded occurrence of Bd in this genus, as well as the first known occurrence of Bd in Alabama (Byrne et al. 2008). While the prevalence of infection in both pickerel frog and Southern two-lined salamander was high (76% and 42%, respectively), no obvious signs of the disease were observed in any infected animals during a routine field examination. Given the large sample sizes of these two species and the high prevalence of infection, a reasonable expectation would be that sampled individuals would present several stages of infection. If the infection had indeed progressed into the disease stage, some characteristics of the disease would be readily identified through field examination (e.g., abnormal ecdysis, or exudates). Our lack of detection of signs of the disease could be attributed to observer error (e.g., unique presentation of the disease in the species, less obvious signs of disease, the infection had not progressed to the disease and no signs existed), but given the extensive physical examination by the SECN field team of all sampled specimens this is not likely.

Due to environmental conditions (i.e., prolonged periods of high temperatures), the fungus is less likely to persist at the southernmost SECN parks (e.g., CANA, CUIS, FOMA, TIMU/FOCA), to have substantial impacts on populations, or to be frequent enough to be detected in low- to medium-intensity surveys (i.e., this survey). The recent findings, however, by Rizkalla (2009, 2010) question this assumption; at least for the SECN parks in northern Florida. Although the fungus was not detected at OCMU, it was detected at Warm Springs National Fish Hatchery approximately 120 km to the west (Green and Dodd 2007). Further, OCMU's geographic location corresponds to a higher probability of fungal presence, as suggested by predictive modeling efforts by Ron (2005), but small sample sizes, particularly for Ranids, may be associated with our lack of detection in our survey (Table 5). Ranids also composed a small proportion of the sample collected at KEMO. The detected occurrence of Bd in one bullfrog sample at KEMO indicates that the fungus is indeed present at KEMO, but our efforts were insufficient at adequately and confidently characterizing its prevalence or host associations (Table 6). A notable concern of this finding at KEMO is that bullfrog is known to host the fungus but does not develop chytridiomycosis (Mazzoni et al. 2003, Daszak et al. 2004), thus serving as a probable transmission vector to other species. Due to the proximity (<24 km apart), general similarities among the natural communities and stressors, and similar amphibian communities at KEMO and CHAT, it is likely similar patterns of Bd occurrences exist at the two parks. Further, the known occurrence of the Bd in the Johnson Ferry Unit at CHAT, a unit not typical of the park as a whole, suggest that broader survey efforts may be necessary to fully understand the distribution and host associations of Bd at this park.

Although Hossack et al. (2010) found low prevalence of Bd in headwater streams (i.e., first- to third-order), our findings of higher prevalence in two species in similar streams at HOBE suggest that associative differences in habitat components (although unknown) between the two studies and study locations likely exist. Latitudinal, stream substrate, weather, and the response of the fungus to these variables–and likely several other unknown/unmentioned factors–also play a role in prevalence, and susceptibility of different species in streams versus wetlands.

It has been suggested that prevalence, and susceptibility, may vary as a function of habitat quality. We agree with this likelihood, but posit that susceptibility would be affected by specific or aggregate effects of factors that degrade amphibian habitat; and aggregate effects indeed seem most logical. Given the dramatic variability in amphibian habitat, these adverse influences and subsequent patterns of susceptibility are likely regional. For example, if specific pollutants degrade the natural defense system via various secretions in amphibian skin, these could be localized. Our detected high prevalence of Bd in two species at HOBE, however, is difficult to explain in this context. HOBE is host to amphibian habitats that are generally accepted to be of high quality. The combination of stressors that increased Bd susceptibility in these two species is ambiguous at best. Very specific habitat components that have yet to be identified may be the catalyst that allows the fungus to perpetuate longer than average or expected until an appropriate host becomes available. Skerratt et al. (2007), however, did find Bd in "pristine" amphibian habitats.

Although Bd is a concern for all SECN parks, amphibian populations at some parks may be at higher risk than others. For example, due to the high ratio of freshwater resources to area at CALO and CAHA, the presence of the fungus here can have significant detrimental impacts on amphibian species that depend on persistent wetlands (e.g., ponds, large wetland complexes) for reproduction; as the aggregation of species increases, the probability of disease transmission also increases. These species may be at higher risk compared to species that utilize ephemeral freshwater resources. Further, pond-breeding species or reservoir hosts [e.g., bullfrog (Mazzoni et al. 2003; Daszak et al. 2004)] may serve as vectors of the fungus to other wetlands or predominantly terrestrial amphibians (Rothermel et al. 2008).

Two parks (i.e., CANA, CALO) were sampled during the summer months when the likelihood of detecting the fungus is the lowest due to seasonal and temperature effects on Bd growth (Piotrowski et al. 2004, Retallick et al. 2004, Kriger and Hero 2006, Kriger and Hero 2007). Rothermel et al. (2008) found no positive results in any samples collected during summer months. Sampling season and small sample sizes for all species in all parks surveyed, as evidenced by low confidence rates for detection probability of the fungus (Table 6), might have increased our false negative rate.

Despite the substantial impacts that Bd has had on members of the family Bufonidae in the western U.S. (Green et al. 2002, Muths et al. 2003, Longcore et al. 2007) and the high frequency of Bd occurrence in the northeastern U.S., we found no evidence of Bd in the 11 Bufonidae samples collected. Our sample size, however, for Bufonidae was small to support a confident determination (Table 6) and warrants supplementation. A similar scenario exists for the detection of Bd in *Lithobates* spp. at CHAT, but the small sample of bullfrog at KEMO also warrants supplementation. As with many infectious diseases, chytridiomycosis may have a profound effect on some species while having little effect on other species (Fisher et al. 2009).

Given the other well known amphibian pathogens, in combination with anthropogenic stressors (e.g., pollutants, habitat loss and aggregated populations; Blaustein and Wake 1990, Carey 1993, Kiesecker et al. 2001, Rohr et al. 2008), it remains unclear if infection probability or individual susceptibility to Bd infection is currently higher than historic levels, or if the Bd pathogen is indeed a new emergence. Museum studies suggest Bd has existed in many locations with current occurrences of Bd during the majority of this century (Ouellet et al. 2005, Garner et al. 2006, Soto-Azat et al. 2010, Reeder et al. 2011). It remains unclear if the pathogen is newly emerged and amphibians have not developed a resistance to it (Rachowicz et al. 2005), if current environmental conditions are more conducive to the proliferation of this pathogen, or if occurrences recently realized are related to increasing survey effort and amphibian-monitoring activities.

A much discussed and debated topic is global climate change and its possible effect on Bd. The expected increased temperature variability associated with climate change is suspected to decrease amphibians' immunity / increase susceptibility to Bd (Raffel et al. 2006) and increase the likelihood of progression of Bd infection to chytridiomycosis (Pounds et al. 2006). Despite the effects climate change will have on Bd, further research is necessary to predict the potential scenarios.

We are in agreement with Rothermel et al. (2008) that predictive modeling efforts, similar to those of Ron (2005), would prove useful if focused on Southeastern U.S. species. Higher resolution geospatial representation of environmental conditions and known Bd niche parameters, and as with Ron (2005), supplemented and refined with known Bd occurrences would further refine our regional understanding and predictive abilities. This may serve as an aid to focus future survey and population-monitoring efforts. Given the possibility of the recent addition (i.e., shortly after the industrial revolution) of anthropogenic stressors to amphibians and their habitats, we also recommend that future predictive modeling incorporate geospatial representations of known and hypothesized stressors (e.g., water quality, water quantity, air quality, deposition rates). Further, the addition of the different forecasted outcomes of climate change would likely prove advantageous to the model's utility. These models will serve as a baseline for the extant distribution of Bd in the Southeast under various stressors and forecasted regimes, and allow managers to develop potential mitigation strategies accordingly.

As expected, the results presented herein generate more questions; particularly regarding the adequacy of the sampling effort and species included in the sample. We recommend targeted population studies on species known to host Bd in areas with confirmed presence and those with no confirmed presence of the pathogen. Because the Southeastern U.S. region shares many of the same species and environmental conditions thought to support the fungus, knowledge of species-specific occurrences and distribution of Bd throughout the region is necessary to focus priorities, objectives, build regional partnerships, and determine the SECN's future sampling efforts (e.g., target species, support of population and disease-effect studies). As with all involved and interested parties, our goal is to provide a solid informational foundation for land managers with known Bd occurrences to collaboratively consider, develop, and evaluate potential management actions to mitigate the negative impacts and, if possible, through habitat management or other means, enhance species' resilience to infection.

Figure 4. Amphibian species testing positive for *Batrachochytrium dendrobatidis* in SECN parks, 2004-2008. Clockwise from top: *Eurycea cirrigera* (southern two-lined salamander; photo by M.W. Byrne), *Lithobates catesbeianus* (bullfrog; photo by J.D. Willson), *Lithobates palustris* (pickerel frog; photo by J.D. Willson), and *Lithobates sphenocephalus* (southern leopard frog; photo by M.W. Byrne). **NOT** actual photos of infected individuals.

Because differential susceptibility remains very unclear, opportunistic surveys by the SECN will continue, either through cooperators or combined with our ongoing Vital Signs monitoring, in SECN parks as travel restrictions and funding allows. This will increase sample sizes and target those species known or suspected to host the fungus (e.g., Ranids, Bufonids, select members of Caudata) and further our understanding of the role of the fungus as Bd hosts are identified in conjunction with community-level data are collected as part of long-term implementation of the SECN amphibian monitoring protocol (Byrne et al., *in preparation*). Although population- and community-level studies in species and locations known to host the fungus would be very beneficial, these studies fall outside the purview and mandate of the SECN's Vital Signs monitoring program, but our existing dataset and resources could prove useful in a collaborative effort.

Management Implications

Although a relationship between the presence of Bd and adversely-impacted populations has not been established in those SECN parks with a known presence of Bd, there is an increasing number of surveys underway in both National Parks nation-wide and non-NPS properties in the southeastern states to further our understanding of the disease and how to manage occurrences in high amphibian-diversity areas. It is important to note, however, that Bd parasitism does not always lead to the death of an individual (i.e., the progression of Bd parasitism to chytridiomycosis; Vazquez et al. 2009, Retalick and Miera 2007, Woodhams and Alford 2004). Further, some individuals can host the fungus without ever developing chytridiomycosis (Vazquez et al. 2009, Daszak et al. 2004). Many of the past amphibian extinctions documented in Central America and Australia did so without prior evidence of Bd presence. However, there has been a subsequent attribution of Bd as the likely causative agent (Berger et al. 1998, Kriger and Hero 2007). Early detection is the key to allow for disease prevention (Boyle et al. 2004) and the lessons learned from the Central American and Australian amphibian losses should serve as a cautionary note.

Because the fungus can persist in an infectious state in surface water for up to seven weeks (Johnson and Speare 2003), sampling a water body of interest directly should also be considered by managers. Quantitative methods have been developed to detect Bd in water and sediments, eliminating invasive sampling of amphibians (Kirshtein et al. 2007, Walker et al. 2007), although estimated to be less than 60% effective (Hossack et al. 2010). These promising new techniques might prove a useful tool in future research to determine Bd's presence in water bodies, focus synoptic studies, and to monitor and predict fungus transmission at population and landscape levels (D. Calhoun, pers. comm.). The ability to detect Bd in the environment and outside the host is critical to predict the possible future impacts and spread of the disease, as samples of the hosts may contain saprophytic stages that are not yet detectable; these stages likely with the ability to multiply (Walker et al. 2007).

The primary tool managers currently have against Bd is increasing public awareness and prevention. The public may be less prone to releasing exotic-pet amphibians on park lands if they are aware of the possible adverse outcomes of the release. Prevention measures also include working with contractors / researchers that are conducting activities in wetlands, ponds, or streams to ensure they follow disinfection procedures (e.g., NSW National Parks and Wildlife Service 2001) for all equipment prior to initiating work.

Although no evidence currently exists that Bd is having an adverse impact on SECN amphibians, some control options are available to avoid the extirpation of a species. These include physical (Woodhams et al. 2003), chemical (Johnson et al. 2003), and possibly forthcoming biological control / bioaugmentation techniques (Brucker et al. 2008; Harris et al. 2009). Chemical controls, however, are currently the most practical and effective technique for field application and include chloramphenicol (Bishop et al. 2009) and didecyl dimethyl ammonium chloride (active ingredient in Path-X™ and quaternary compound 128; Johnson et al. 2003). Application of chemical disinfectants, however, involves the capture of individuals, which can be expensive, and the efficacy of these techniques on the restoration of a persistent population remains unknown. Further, this technique only treats the individual infections and not the system, so viable Bd zoospores will likely remain. We do not recommend pursuing control actions at this time.

The biological control / bioaugmentation of Bd is promising but in its infancy. Recent discoveries of naturally-occurring antifungal bacteria in amphibians that survived local Bd outbreaks (Brucker et al. 2008, Harris et al. 2009) may lead to new, inexpensive, and highly effective techniques to combat the fungus.

If Bd is detected in a population, and established to have an adverse impact, there are currently no realistic (i.e., affordable, logistically sound, proven effective, practical) strategies for remediation or guarantees that future infection of treated individuals will not occur. Treatment becomes more complex in areas with high amphibian-species diversity, a characteristic of all SECN parks, because of potential differential effects on species within the local amphibian community. Given the international attention Bd has received, however, the increase in research and monitoring internationally, and improved collaboration, promising new discoveries are frequent and our knowledge of the fungus is rapidly increasing. These efforts have resulted in several management strategies for infected populations, with varied levels of success and cost, and the beginning of a compendium of lessons learned. Continued collaboration is the key to our success at developing effective mitigation strategies for the perpetuation of infected populations.

Literature Cited

ASIH / HL / SSAR (The American Society of Ichthyologists and Herpetologists / The Herpetologist's League / The Society for the Study of Amphibians and Reptiles). 2004. Guidelines for use of live amphibians and reptiles in field and laboratory research, 2nd ed. Available online (www.asih.org/files/hacc-final.pdf).

Bakkegard, K.A. and A.P. Pessier. 2010. *Batrachochytrium dendrobatidis* in Adult *Notophthalmus viridescens* in North-Central Alabama, USA. Herpetological Review 41:45-47.

Berger, L., R. Speare, P. Daszak, E. Green, A. A. Cunningham, C. L. Goggin, R. Slocombe, M. A. Ragan, A. D. Hyatt, K. R. McDonald, H. B. Hines, K. R. Lips, G. Marantelli, and H. Parkes. 1998. Chytridiomycosis causes amphibian mortality associated with population declines in the rain forests of Australia and Central America. Proceedings of the National Academy of Sciences USA 95:9031–9036.

Bishop, P. J., R. Speare, R. Poulter, M. Butler, B. J. Speare, A. Hyatt, V. Olsen, and A. Haigh. 2009. Elimination of the amphibian chytrid fungus *Batrachochytrium dendrobatidis* by Archey's frog *Leiopelma archeyi*. Diseases of Aquatic Organisms 84:9-15.

Blaustein, A. R. and D. B. Wake. 1990. Declining amphibians: A global phenomenon? Trends in Ecology and Evolution 5:203-204.

Boyle, D. G., B. B. Boyle, V. Olsen, J. A. T. Morgan, and A. D. Hyatt. 2004. Rapid quantitative detection of chytridiomycosis (*Batrachochytrium dendrobatidis*) in amphibian samples using real-time Taqman PCR assay. Diseases of Aquatic Organisms 60:141-148.

Briggler, J., K. A. Larson, and K. J. Irwin. 2008. Presence of the amphibian chytrid fungus (*Batrachochytrium dendrobatidis*) on Hellbenders (*Cryptobranchus alleganiensis*) in the Ozark highlands. Herpetological Review 39:443-444.

Briggs C. J., V. T. Vredenburg, R. A. Knapp, and L. J. Rachowicz. 2005. Investigating the population-level effects of chytridiomycosis: an emerging infectious disease of amphibians. Ecology 86:3149-3159.

Brucker R. M., R. N. Harris, C. R. Schwantes, T. N. Gallaher, D. C. Flaherty, B. A. Lam, K. P. Minbiole. 2008. Amphibian chemical defense: antifungal metabolites of the microsymbiont *Janthinobacterium lividum* on the salamander *Plethodon cinereus*. Journal of Chemical Ecology 34:1422–1429.

Byrne, M. W., L. M. Elston, and B. D. Smrekar. *In preparation*. Draft amphibian community monitoring in Southeast Coast Network parks. USDI National Park Service, Southeast Coast Network, Atlanta, GA, USA.

Byrne, M. W., E. D. Davie, and J. W. Gibbons. 2008. *Batrachochytrium dendrobatidis* occurrence in *Eurycea cirrigera*. Southeastern Naturalist 7:551-555.

Byrne, M. W. 2007. Standard Operating Procedure #8: Chytrid fungus (Bd) sampling. *In* Byrne et al., *in preparation*, Draft amphibian community monitoring in Southeast Coast Network parks. Southeast Coast Network, Inventory and Monitoring Program, National Park Service, Atlanta, GA, USA.

Carey, C. 1993. Hypothesis concerning the causes of the disappearance of boreal toads from the mountains of Colorado. Conservation Biology 7:355-362.

Chatfield, M. W., B. B. Rothermel, C. S. Brooks, and J. B. Kay. 2009. Detection of *Batrachochytrium dendrobatidis* in amphibians from the Great Smoky Mountains of North Carolina and Tennessee, USA. Herpetological Review 40:176-179.

Chinnadurai, S. K. D. Cooper, D. S. Dombrowski, M. F. Poore, and M. G. Levy. 2009. Experimental infection of native North Carolina salamanders with *Batrachochytrium dendrobatidis*. Journal of Wildlife Diseases 45:631-636.

Cummer, M. R., D. E. Green, and E. M. O'Neill. 2005. Aquatic chytrid pathogen detected in terrestrial plethodontid salamander. Herpetological Review 36:248-249.

Daszak P., A. A. Cunningham, and A. D. Hyatt. 2003. Infectious disease and amphibian population declines. Diversity and Distributions 9:141-150.

Daszak, P., A. Strieby, A. A. Cunningham, J. E. Longcore, C. C. Brown, and D. Porter. 2004. Experimental evidence that the bullfrog (*Lithobates catesbeiana*) is a potential carrier of chytridiomycosis, an emerging fungal disease of amphibians. Herpetological Journal 14:201-207.

Di Rosa, I., F. Simoncelli, A. Fagotti, and R. Pascolini. 2007. Ecology: The proximate cause of frog declines? Nature 447:E4-E5.

DiGiacomo, R. F, and T. D. Koepsell. 1986. Sampling for detection of infection or disease in animal populations. Journal of the American Veterinary Medical Association 189:22-23.

Duellman, W.E. and L. Trueb. 1986. Biology of Amphibians. McGraw-Hill, New York, New York, USA. 670 pp.

Echternacht, A. C. and L. D. Harris. 1993. The fauna and wildlife of the southeastern United States. Biodiversity of the Southeastern United States: lowland terrestrial communities (eds. W. H. Martin, S. G. Boyce & A. C. Echternacht), pp. 81-116. John Wiley & Sons, New York, New York, USA.

Fisher, M., T. Garner, and S. Walker. 2009. Global emergence of *Batrachochytrium dendrobatidis* and amphibian chytridiomycosis in space, time, and host. Microbiology 63:291.

Garner T. W. J., M. Perkins, P. Govindarajulu, D. Seglie, S. J. Walker, A. A. Cunningham, and M. C. Fisher. 2006. The emerging amphibian pathogen *Batrachochytrium dendrobatidis* globally infects introduced populations of the North American bullfrog, *Rana catesbeiana*. Biological Letters 2:455-459.

Gonynor, J. L, M. J. Yabsley and J. B. Jensen. 2011. A Preliminary Survey of Batrachochytrium dendrobatidis Exposure in Hellbenders from a Stream in Georgia, USA. Herpetological Review 42:58-59

Green, D. E., K. A. Converse, and A. K. Schrader. 2002. Epizootiology of sixty-four amphibian morbidity and mortality events in the USA, 1996-2001. Annals of the New York Academy of Sciences 969:323-339.

Green D. E., and C. K. Dodd, Jr. 2007. Presence of amphibian chytrid fungus *Batrachochytrium dendrobatidis* and other amphibian pathogens at warmwater fish hatcheries in southeastern North America. Herpetological Conservation and Biology 2:43-47.

Harris R. N., R. M. Brucker, J. B. Walke, M. H. Becker, C. R. Schwantes, D. C. Flaherty, B. A. Lam, D. C. Woodhams, C. J. Briggs, V. T. Vredenburg, and K. P. Minbiole. 2009. Skin microbes on frogs prevent morbidity and mortality caused by a lethal skin fungus. International Society for Microbial Ecology Journal 3:818-824.

Hossack B. R., E. Muths, C. W. Anderson, J. D. Kirshtein, and P. S. Corn. 2009. Distribution limits of Batrachochytrium dendrobatidis: a case study in the Rocky Mountains, USA. Journal of Wildlife Diseases 45:1198-1202.

Hossack, B. R., M. J. Adams, E. H. C. Grant, C. A. Pearl, J. B. Bettaso, W. J. Barichivich, W. H. Lowe, K. True, J. L. Ware, and P. S. Corn. 2010. Rarity of pathogenic chytrid fungus (*Batrachochytrium dendrobatidis*) in headwater amphibians of the USA. Journal of Herpetology 52:253-260.

Johnson, M. L, L. Berger, L. Philips, and R. Speare. 2003. Fungicidal effects of chemical disinfectants, UV light, desiccation and heat on the amphibian chytrid *Batrachochytrium dendrobatidis*. Diseases of Aquatic Organisms 57:255-260.

Johnson, M. L., and R. Speare. 2003. Survival of *Batrachochytrium dendrobatidis* in water: Quarantine and disease control implications. Emerging Infectious Diseases 9:922-925.

Kiesecker, J. M., A. R. Blaustein, and L. K. Belden. 2001. Complex causes of amphibian population declines. Nature 410:681-684.

Kilpatrick A. M., C. J. Briggs, P. Daszak. 2010. The ecology and impact of chytridiomycosis: An emerging disease of amphibians. Trends in Ecology and Evolution25:109-118.

Kirshtein J. D., C. W. Anderson, J. S. Wood, J. E. Longcore, and M. A. Voytek. 2007. Quantitative PCR detection of *Batrachochytrium dendrobatidis* DNA from sediments and water. Diseases of Aquatic Organisms 77:11-15.

Kriger K. M, and J. M. Hero. 2006. Large-scale seasonal variation in the prevalence and severity of chytridiomycosis. Journal of Zoology 271: 352–359.

Kriger, K. M., and J. M. Hero. 2007. The chytrid fungus *Batrachochytrium dendrobatidis* is non-randomly distributed across amphibian breeding habitats. Diversity and Distributions 13:781-788.

Lips, K. R., J. D. Reeve, and L. Witters. 2003. Ecological traits predicting amphibian population declines in Central America. Conservation Biology 17: 1078–1088

Lips, K. R., F. Brem, R. Brenes, J. D. Reeve, R. A. Alford, J. Voyles, C. Carey, L. Livo, A. P. Pessier, and J. C. Collins. 2006. Emerging infectious disease and the loss of biodiversity in a Neotropical amphibian community. Proceedings of the National Academy of Sciences of the United States of America 103: 3165-3170.

Longcore, J. R., J. E. Longcore, A. P. Pessier, and W. A. Halteman. 2007. Chytridiomycosis widespread in anurans of northeastern United States. Journal of Wildlife Management 71:435-444.

Longcore, J. E., A. P. Pessier, and D. K. Nichols. 1999. *Batrachochytrium dendrobatidis* gen. et sp. nov., a chytrid pathogenic to amphibians. Mycologia 91:219–227.

Mazzoni, R., A. A. Cunningham, P. Daszak, A. Apolo, E. Perdomo, and G. Speranza. 2003. Emerging pathogen of wild amphibians in frogs (*Lithobates catesbeiana*) farmed for international trade. Emerging Infectious Diseases 9:995–998.

Mitchell J. C. and D. E. Green. 2002. Chytridiomycosis in two species of ranid frogs in the southeastern United States. Joint Meeting of the American Society of Ichthyologists and Herpetologists, Herpetologists' League, and Society for the Study of Amphibians and Reptiles, 4-8 July 2002, Kansas City, USA.

Mitchell, K. M., T. S. Churcher, T. W. J. Garner, and M. C. Fisher. 2008. Persistence of the emerging pathogen Batrachochytrium dendrobatidis outside the amphibian host greatly increases the probability of host extinction. Proceedings of the Royal Society B: Biological Sciences 275:329-334.

Montanucci, R.R. 2009. The chytrid fungus in the Red Salamander, Pseudotriton ruber, in South Carolina, USA. Herpetological Review 40:188.

Muths, E., P. S. Corn, A. P. Pessier, D. E. Green. 2003. Evidence for disease-related amphibian decline in Colorado. Biological Conservation 110:357-365.

NPSpecies - The National Park Service Biodiversity Database. Secure online version. https://science1.nature.nps.gov/npspecies/web/main/start (Park list: accessed 3/1/2011)

NSW National Parks and Wildlife Service. 2001. Hygiene protocol for the control of disease in frogs. Information Circular Number 6. NSW NPWS, Hurstville NSW, Australia.

Ouellet M., I. Mikaelian, B. D. Pauli, J. Rodrigue, and D. M. Green. 2005. Historical evidence for widespread chytrid infection in North American amphibian populations. Conservation Biology 19:1431-1440

Petersen, C., R. E. Lovich, M. J. Lannoo, and P. Nanjappa. 2011. Do frogs still get their kicks on Route 66? A transcontinental transect for amphibian chytrid fungus (*Batrachochytrium dendrobatidis*) infection on U.S Department of Defense Installations. Project Number (09-426). Final Report, February, 2011.

Peterson J. D., M. B. Wood, W. A. Hopkins, J. M Unrine, and M. T. Mendonça. 2007. Prevalence of *Batrachochytrium dendrobatidis* in American bullfrog and southern leopard frog larvae from wetlands on the Savannah River Site, South Carolina. Journal of Wildlife Disease 43:450-460.

Petranka, J. W. 1998. Salamanders of the United States and Canada. Smithsonian Institution Press, Washington, DC, USA.

Piotrowski J. S., S. L. Annis, and J. F. Longcore . 2004. Physiology of Batrachochytrium dendrobatidis, a chytrid pathogen of amphibians. Mycologia 96: 9-15.

Pounds, J. A., M. R. Bustamante, L. A. Coloma, J. A. Consuegra, M. P. L. Fogden, P. N. Foster, E. La Marca, K. L. Masters, A. Merino-Viteri, R. Puschendorf, S. R. Ron, G. A. Sanchez-Azofeifa, C. J. Still, and B. E. Young. 2006. Widespread amphibian extinctions from epidemic disease driven by global warming. Nature 439:161–167.

Rachowicz, L. J., J. Hero, R. A. Alford, J. W. Taylor, J. A. T. Morgan, V. T. Vrendenberg, J. P. Collins, and C. J. Briggs. 2005. The novel and endemic pathogen hypotheses: Competing explanations for the origin of emerging infectious diseases of wildlife. Conservation Biology 19:1441-1448.

Raffel T. R., J. R. Rohr, J. M. Kiesecker, and P. J. Hudson. 2006. Negative effects of changing temperature on amphibian immunity under field conditions. Functional Ecol 20:819-828.

Reeder, N. M. M., T. L. Cheng, V.T. Vredenburg, and D.C. Blackburn. 2011. Survey of the chytrid fungus Batrachochytrium dendrobatidis from montane and lowland frogs in eastern Nigeria. Herpetology Notes 4:83-86.

Retallick R.W.R., H. McCallum, R. Speare. 2004. Endemic infection of the amphibian chytrid fungus in a frog community post-decline. PLOS Biol 2: e351. doi:10.1371/journal.pbio.0020351

Retallick R. W. R., and V. Miera. 2007. Strain differences in the amphibian chytrid *Batrachochytrium dendrobatidis* and non-permanent, sub-lethal effects of infection. Diseases of Aquatic Organisms 75:201-207.

Rizkalla, C. E. 2009. First reported detection of *Batrachochytrium dendrobatidis* in Florida, USA. Herpetological Review 40:189-190.

Rizkalla, C. E. 2010. Increasing detections of Batrachochytrium dendrobatidis in Central Florida, USA. Herpetological Review 41:180-181.

Rohr, J. R., T. R. Raffel, J. M. Romansic, H. McCallum, and P. J. Hudson. 2008. Evaluating the links between climate, disease spread, and amphibian declines. Proceedings of the National Academy of Science 105:17436–17441.

Rohr, J. R., and T. R. Raffel. 2010. Linking global climate and temperature variability to widespread amphibian declines putatively caused by disease. Proceedings of the National Academy of Sciences (USA). 107:8269-8274.

Ron, S. R. 2005. Predicting the distribution of the amphibian pathogen *Batrachochytrium dendrobatidis* in the New World. Biotropica 37:209–221.

Rothermel B. B., S.C. Walls, J. C. Mitchell, C. K. Dodd, Jr., L. K. Irwin, D. E. Green, V. M Vazquez, J. W. Petranka, and D. J. Stevenson. 2008. Widespread occurrence of the amphibian chytrid fungus *Batrachochytrium dendrobatidis* in amphibian populations in the southeastern USA. Diseases of Aquatic Organisms 82:3-18.

Skerratt L. F., L. Berger, R. Speare, S. Cashins, K. R. McDonald, A. D Phillott, H. B. Hines, and N. Kenyon. 2007. Spread of chytridiomycosis has caused the rapid global decline and extinction of frogs. EcoHealth: DOI:10.1007/s10393-10007-10093-10395.

Soto-Azat, C., B. T. Clarke, J. C. Poynton, and A. A. Cunningham. 2010. Widespread historical presence of Batrachochytrium dendrobatidis in African pipid frogs. Diversity and Distributions 16:126-131.

Timpe, E. K., S. P. Graham, R. W. Gagliardo,R. L. Hill, and M. G. Levy. 2008. Occurrence of the fungal pathogen *Batrachochytrium dendrobatidis* in Georgia's Amphibian populations. Herpetological Review 39:447-449.

Tobler U., and B. R. Schmidt. 2010. Within- and among-population variation in chytridiomycosis-induced mortality in the toad *Alytes obstetricans*. PLoS ONE 5:e10927. doi:10.1371/journal.pone.0010927.

Todd-Thompson, M., D. L. Miller, P. E. Super and M. J. Gray. 2009. Chytridiomycosis-associated mortality in a *Rana palustris* collected in Great Smoky Mountains National Park, Tennessee, USA. Herpetological Review. 40:321-323.

Tuberville, T. D., J. D. Willson, M. E. Dorcas, and J. W. Gibbons. 2005. Herpetofaunal species richness of southeastern national parks. Southeastern Naturalist 4:537-569.

Vazquez, V.M., B. B. Rothermel, and A.P. Pessier. 2009. Experimental infection of North American plethodontid salamanders with the fungus *Batrachochytrium dendrobatidis*. Diseases of Aquatic Organisms 84:1–7.

Venesky, M. D. and F. M. Brem. 2008. Occurrence of *Batrachochytrium dendrobatidis* in the southwestern Tennessee, USA. Herpetological Review 39:319-320.

Voyles, J., L. Berger, S. Young,, R. Speare,R. Webb,, and J. Warner. 2007. Electrolyte depletion and osmotic imbalance in amphibians with chytridiomycosis. Diseases of Aquatic Organisms 77:113-118.

Voyles, J., S. Young, L. Berger, C. Campbell, W. F. Voyles, A. Dinudom, D. Cook, R. Webb, R. A. Alford, L. F. Skerratt, and R. Speare. 2009. Pathogenesis of Chytridiomycosis, a Cause of Catastrophic Amphibian Declines. Science 326:582-585.

Walker S. F, M. B. Salas, D. Jenkins, T. W. J. Garner, A. A. Cunningham, A. D. Hyatt, J. Bosch, and M. C. Fisher. 2007. Environmental detection of *Batrachochytrium dendrobatidis* in a temperate climate. Diseases of Aquatic Organisms 77:102–112.

Woodhams, D. C., R. A. Alford, and G. Marantelli. 2003. Emerging disease of amphibians cured by elevated body temperature. Diseases of Aquatic Organisms 55:65-67.

Woodhams, D. C., and R. A. Alford. 2004. Ecology of chytridiomycosis in rainforest stream frog assemblages of tropical Queensland. Conservation Biology 19:1449-1459.

Woodhams, D. C., K. Ardipradja, R. A. Alford, G. Marantelli, L.K. Reinert, L. A. Rollins-Smith. 2007. Resistance to chytridiomycosis varies among amphibian species and is correlated with skin peptide defenses. Animal Conservation 10:409-417.

NPS 964/109152, August 2011